THE REPUBLICAN
JOKE BOOK

——— ★ ———

FUN POLITICAL HUMOR, PUNS AND
JOKES FOR REPUBLICANS

Wayne Smith

ISBN: 979-8-88768-021-7
Copyright © 2024 by Red Panda Press
ALL RIGHTS RESERVED

★ CONTENTS ★

★ WELCOME ★

Hello and welcome to the Republican Joke Book. At the time of publishing this book, we're staring down the barrel of yet another nail-biting US election! Moving on from the 2020 election between Donald Trump and Joe Biden, we're looking to the future and the candidates are... Donald Trump and Joe Biden?

Well, perhaps. As of the start of 2024, it's not yet clear who the candidates are going to be, but there's a strong chance it'll be the same as before. At this rate, there's a genuine chance that Julius Caesar will be reanimated and join the running as an independent, keep an eye on that story as it develops.

Either way, we can have a brilliant laugh at it all.

This book is quite simply a selection of jokes, jokettes, parodies, satirical comments, and other silly things that will make you **a Republican** laugh. Throughout, you'll notice that the humorous content is divided into chapters so you can choose what flavor of laughter you're after. It also means if you're unable to laugh at yourself, you can avoid the chapter about laughing other Republicans.

In this book you'll find a ton of material that pokes fun at liberals, woke-ism, elections, politicians, presidents, and of course Democrats. With any luck you'll find plenty within these pages that's worth laughing at, and you hereby have the author's permission to use these jokes at parties and pretend you came up with them.

Even better, if you use the jokes at the right fundraising event, you may very well be elected for local government.

It's worth saying that if you don't have a sense of humor, it's best that you turn back now. If you can't take a joke pointed towards America's greatest (and worst) presidents, then grow a funny bone and come back when you stop being so boring. This book is designed to be a laugh; if you don't like one of the jokes then move on and see if you like the one after that. Or you can "X" your outrage on Twitter, or tweet your outrage on X, whichever way round you like (thanks Elon) and become yet another raging keyboard warrior – it's up to you.

Hopefully you find time in between rage-tweeting to have a right giggle at the silly material in these pages and enjoy some light-hearted Republican jokes. It's a dicey time in America politically, so it helps to take a step back and laugh at how absurd it can all get.

Here's an *amuse bouche*, a taster:

What's the best thing about being Joe Biden?

Waking up every day and learning that you're President.

"The 2024 Presidential Race"

SPEECHES TO HELP WITH WOKING THE BEAR

History is full of some exceptional speeches from amazing orators, politicians, activists, and all sorts of people from all walks of life.

Unfortunately, however, they sometimes weren't the most politically correct of speeches, so our speech editor Dr Wokenstein is going to go through some of the most famous ones and edit them to be a bit more inclusive and inoffensive.

You should be grateful – it's difficult to get hold of Dr Wokenstein nowadays, they're very busy!

Enjoy reading some of the world's best known speeches, now made woke-r and more acceptable for the delicate ears of the 21st century. You'll undoubtedly agree that they're tons better for it.

Winston Churchill, The Finest Hour, 1940.

"We shall go on to the end, we shall ~~fight~~ **gently engage** in France, we shall ~~fight~~ **ask the Germans to stop** on the seas and oceans, we shall ~~fight with growing confidence and growing strength in the air~~ **send a strongly worded letter**, we shall defend our Island, <u>whatever</u> the cost may be **unless it means we have to get up before 10pm**. We shall ~~fight on~~ **travel to** the beaches, we shall ~~fight~~ **tut** on the landing grounds, we shall ~~fight~~ **meditate** in the fields and in ~~the streets~~ **communes**, we shall ~~fight~~ **play** in the hills; we shall never surrender! **<u>Unless, of course, that would make the Nazis happy.</u>**"

***

Theodore Roosevelt, "Duties of American Citizenship," 1883.

"No ~~man~~ **person** can be a good citizen who is not a good ~~husband~~ **member of a thruple** and a good ~~father~~ **co-parent**, who is not honest in ~~his~~ **their** dealings with other men and women **and transwomen and transmen**, faithful to ~~his~~ **their** friends and fearless in the presence of ~~his~~ **their** foes, who has not got a sound heart, a ~~sound~~ **leftie** mind, and a sound body..."

"~~Tell General Howard I know his heart. What he told me before, I have it in my heart. I am tired of fighting. Our Chiefs are killed; Looking Glass is dead, Ta Hool Hool Shute is dead. The old men are all dead. It is the young men who say yes or no. He who led on the young men is dead. It is cold, and we have no blankets; the little children are freezing to death. My people, some of them, have run away to the hills, and have no blankets, no food. No one knows where they are - perhaps freezing to death. I want to have time to look for my children, and see how many of them I can find. Maybe I shall find them among the dead. Hear me, my Chiefs! I am tired; my heart is sick and sad. From where the sun now stands I will fight no more forever.~~ **White Americans in the 21st century need to apologise, that's exactly what I want.**"

Chief Joseph, "Surrender Speech", 1877.

***

"That ~~man~~ **them** over there says that ~~women~~ **whomever** need to be helped into carriages, and lifted over ditches, and to have the best place everywhere.

Nobody ever helps me into carriages, or over mud-puddles, or gives me any best place! And ain't I a woman? **Or a man if I say I am? Or They?** Look at me! Look at my arm! I have ploughed and planted, and gathered into barns, and no ~~man~~ **they** could head me! And ain't I a ~~woman~~ **they**? I could work as much and eat as much as a man – when I could get it – and bear the lash as well!"

Sojourner Truth, "Ain't I a Woman", 1851.

"Yesterday, December 7, 1941—a date which will live in infamy—the United States of America was suddenly and deliberately attacked by the naval and air forces of the Empire of Japan. **And if they apologise, then we can have a proper discussion about this and put it behind us.**"

Franklin D. Roosevelt, "Dar of Infamy", 1941.

***

"3: ~~Blessed~~ **Empowered** are the poor in spirit: for theirs is the kingdom of heaven **or any other non-denominational post-life area**.

4: ~~Blessed~~ **Empowered** are they that mourn **systemic injustices**: for they shall be comforted.

5: ~~Blessed~~ **Empowered** are the meek: for they shall inherit the earth.

6: ~~Blessed~~ **Empowered** are they which do hunger and thirst after righteousness: for they shall be filled.

7: ~~Blessed~~ **Empowered** are the merciful: for they shall obtain mercy.

8: ~~Blessed~~ **Empowered** are the pure in heart: for they shall see God.

9: ~~Blessed~~ **Empowered** are the peacemakers: for they shall be called the children of God.

10: ~~Blessed~~ **Empowered** are they which are persecuted for righteousness' sake: for theirs is the kingdom of heaven.

P.S. I hope you enjoyed all the gender neutral terms, I use them all the time."

Jesus of Nazareth, "Sermon on the Mount"

---★---

DEMOCRATS

Chances are, if you're reading this silly book, you're a Republican. As a result, you probably don't like Democrats very much. So it feels only fitting to spend this chapter telling some very funny and very silly jokes about Democrats. Feel free to tell these to your Democrat work friend and laugh as they fail to understand any of them.

A devoted Republican man, John, is on his deathbed, having suffered a long battle with illness. He phones his friend, David, with minutes left to live.

"David, I just wanted to let you know that I'm becoming a Democrat."

"Oh gosh, John! Why on earth are you doing that?"

"Because I'd rather one of them die than one of us!"

***

Q: What do you get when you offer a Democrat a penny for their thoughts?

A: Change.

***

Q: What's the difference between a Democrat on a motorcycle and a vacuum cleaner?

A: The vacuum has the dirt bag on the outside.

***

At Church on a Sunday, a local man by the name of Ken announces that his friend, Paul, had died on the weekend. A devoted Democrat, he was beloved by his community, and his family were asking for $10 contributions to pay for the burial.

Ken brings the gift basket to the front row and sees an elderly woman bringing out a $100 bill.

"One hundred dollars? That's a lot of money, I don't know if we can take that!"

"Well, if you can bury one Democrat for $10, then quickly take this and bury nine more!"

Q: What do you call a basement full of Democrats?

A: A Whine Cellar

***

I had an uncle who lived in Chicago, and he had voted Republican all his life. He passed away a few years ago and now he votes Democrat.

***

Q: What's a Democrat's favorite dessert?

A: Im-peach cobbler

***

Q: What's a Democrat's favorite maneuver while driving?

A: The U-Turn

***

Q: How do you confuse a Democrat?

A: You don't. They're born that way.

***

Q: How many Democrats does it take to change a lightbulb?

A: None, they just **talk** about how important it is to change it.

If there weren't any Democrats, then who would be left?

***

It was so cold this morning that I saw a Democrat with his hand in his own pocket!

***

Q: Why do Democrats keep pushing for more gun control?

A: Because they can't stop shooting themselves in the foot!

***

A man walks into a store and sees three brains for sale behind the counter.

The first is a Libertarian brain, priced at $250.
The second is a Republican brain, priced at $275.
The third is a Democratic brain, priced at $5,000,000.

Confused, the man asks why the Democratic brain is so much more expensive than the other two.

The clerk replies, "Well sir, that brain has never been used."

***

A Democrat walks into a bar and asks the bartender, "what's your most popular drink?"

The bartender replies, "A Russian Collusion."

The Democrat responds, "I'll have one of those!"

The bartender hands the Democrat an empty glass and says, "Enjoy."

***

Q: What is foreplay for a Democrat?

A: Thirty minutes of begging.

Have you heard? Starbucks are offering a new drink to honor Nancy Pelosi.

They're calling it the fullacrapuccino.

***

Q: What happens when you cross a pig with a Democrat?

A: Nothing. There are some things that a pig just won't do.

***

A Democrat walks into a doctor's office with a disgusting toad sat on his head.

The toad looks at the doctor and says, "Hey doc, can you get this wart off my ass?"

***

Joe Biden is being briefed by his staff on one cold Monday morning. After fielding his staff's concerns on domestic policy and ideas on how to re-energize the economy, he hears about international defence and conflict.

An aide tells him that following US intervention in South America, significant damage was caused to infrastructure and three Brazilians lost their lives.

Biden turns from the group, aghast. He walks to the window, and the staff look at each other stunned, wondering what brought on this level of emotion in the elderly statesman.

Biden slowly turns around to address the group...

"Okay, how many is a Brazlian?"

Q: How do you know that Democrats are a diverse group of people?

A: Because they keep count of how many people they know in each racial or ethnic category.

***

Q: What do you get when you cross a pilgrim with a Democrat?

A: A god-fearing tax collector who gives thanks for what other people have.

NO TIME LIKE THE PRESIDENT!

In this part of the book we'll take time to have a pop at the most powerful person (it's only been a man so far, but maybe one day it won't be, so I'm saying person for re-readability) in the world. Some jokes will be at specific presidents, while others are more general, but hopefully you'll find time to have a right giggle at the leader of the Land of the Free.

Remember, you can laugh at the president as much as you like! We haven't had a president that's been able to hear you for almost a decade.

Many jokes are like US Presidents

This one is awful.

***

If alive, Steve Jobs would have made a better president than Trump.

But that's comparing Apples to Oranges.

Four former US presidents are caught in a horrible tornado that hits a state funeral they're all attending in Kansas.

Suddenly, all of them are blown off to Oz.

They finally make it to the Emerald City and come before the Great and Powerful Oz.

"What brings you before the great Wizard of Oz?"

Jimmy Carter steps forward timidly. "I've come for some courage."

"No problem!" says the Wizard. "Who is next?"

Ronald Reagan steps forward. "Well...I...I think I need a heart."

"Done!" says the Wizard. "Who comes next before the Great and Powerful Oz?"

Up steps George W. Bush, who says, "I'm told by the American people that I need a brain."

"Not a problem!" says the Wizard. "Consider it done."

There is a prolonged silence in the hall.

Bill Clinton is just standing there, looking around, but doesn't say a word.

Irritated, the Wizard finally asks, "What do you want?"

"Ummm," he says quietly, "is Dorothy around?"

Hillary Clinton is surprisingly elected president in 2024 after demolishing the other candidates. On her first night in the White House, she is visited by the ghost of George Washington.

She asks him, "George, what can I do to best serve the United States?"

The ghost of George Washington responds, "Never tell a lie."

She says, "Oh, I don't think I can do that."

The next night, she is visited by the ghost of Thomas Jefferson. She asks him, "Thomas, what can I do to best serve the United States?"

The ghost of Thomas Jefferson responds, "Listen to the people."

She says, "Oh, I don't think I can do that."

On the third night, she is visited by the ghost of Abraham Lincoln. She asks him, "Abraham, what can I do to best serve the United States?"

The ghost of Abraham Lincoln responds, "Go see a play."

***

President Joe Biden just had a meeting with the cabinet.

Now he's talking to the couch.

***

When I was a little boy, my Dad taught me that any little girl or boy, anyone at all, could grow up to become the president someday.

And I'm starting to believe him.

All these American presidents are so corrupt!

Except for Abraham Lincoln, he was in a cent.

***

Flying across the country in Air Force One, the president jokes with his staff.

"I'm thinking about tossing a $100 bill out the window and making someone very happy."

A White House aide comments, "Why don't you throw twenty $100 bills out the window and make twenty people happy?"

Another staffer jokes, "Why don't you throw a hundred $100 bills out the window and make a hundred people happy?"

A member of the plane staff, wanting to get in on the act, chimes in and says, "Why don't you throw yourself out the window and make half the country happy?"

***

It's interesting to see how different US presidents look at the end of their presidency. Obama had gray hair, Bush had a bunch of wrinkles, and by the end of JFK's presidency, half of his head was missing.

Barack Obama walks into a bar, but he is invisible.

After somehow attracting the bartender's attention, the bartender says, "Okay, I'll bite. Why are you invisible?"

Barack says "Well, I found a bottle on the beach and...then I rubbed it. And then...importantly...A genie came out. The genie said I could have...three wishes."

For my first wish, I said, "Let me say this, and this is profoundly important...I want Michelle to marry me...I love her...and I think America will love her too." That wish was granted.

For my second wish, I said, "Like all patriotic Americans, I am deeply patriotic...and I want to be President...of the United States... so I can serve my country." That wish was granted too.

And then, for my third wish, I started by saying, "Let me be clear..."

***

Back in the early 2000s a group of Marines comes across one of their own laying on one side of the road, and an Iraqi soldier laying on the other side of the road.

When they asked him what happened, the injured Marine explained, "We saw each other, pulled our guns and I shouted "Sadam Hussein sucks!" at the same time he shouted "George Bush sucks!" and we were shaking hands in the road when this truck comes by and runs us both over."

President Clinton and a Secret Service agent go for the president's morning run. While on the run, the Secret Service agent realizes that Bill has a dog with him.

"Is that a new dog Mr. President?"

"Yes," says Bill. "I got it for Hillary."

"Good trade Mr. President, good trade."

***

Former President Trump was asked what the "J" stood for in "Donald J. Trump", and he responded "Genius."

"The most tech-wise politician in Washington!"

And it's in color now!

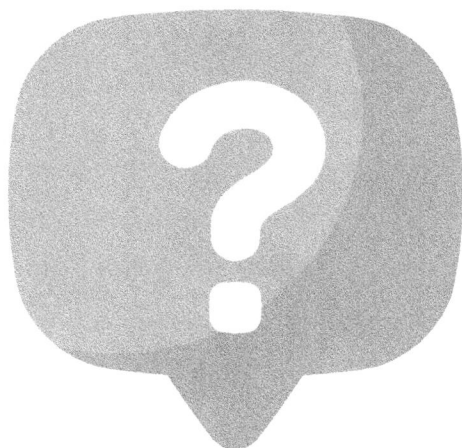

---- ★ ----

GUESS WHO!

In a strange version of the classic game "Guess Who!" you will be presented with a wonderfully out-of-touch quote from a prominent US politician and tasked with identifying who said it!

The answers will be at the end of the chapter. No peeking or you're a smelly communist! (I'm joking!)

1.

"Too many good docs are getting out of the business. Too many OB-GYNs aren't able to practice their love with women all across this country."

Kamala Harris	George W. Bush	Ronald Reagan

2.

"Facts are stupid things."

Ronald Reagan	Barack Obama	George H. W. Bush

3.

"I've now been in 57 states – I think one left to go."

Ronald Reagan	Barack Obama	George H. W. Bush

4.

"Rarely is the question asked: Is our children learning?"

George W. Bush	Ted Cruz	Dick Cheney

5.

"We had no domestic attacks under Bush; we've had one under Obama."

Ron DeSantis	Rudy Giuliani	Ted Kennedy

6.

"One word sums up probably the responsibility of any vice president, and that one word is 'to be prepared'."

Mike Pence	Walter Mondale	Dan Quayle

7.

"We know there are known knowns: there are things we know we know. We also know there are known unknowns: that is to say we know there are things we know we don't know. But there are also unknown unknowns — the ones we don't know we don't know."

Donald Rumsfeld	Dick Cheney	Barack Obama

8.

"I actually did vote for the $87 billion, before I voted against it."

Bill Frist	John Kerry	Barack Obama

9.

"You cannot be President of the United States if you don't have faith. Remember Lincoln, going to his knees in times of trial and the Civil War and all that stuff. You can't be. And we are blessed. So don't feel sorry for – don't cry for me, Argentina. Message: I care."

George H. W. Bush	George W. Bush	Rush Limbaugh

10.
"I have brought tremendous experience and have tremendous tentacles and commitment to this community."

Mitt Romney	Jeb Bush	Karen Handel

11.
"Please clap."

Mitt Romney	Jeb Bush	Karen Handel

12.
"When the President does it, that means it is not illegal."

George W. Bush	Richard Nixon	Lyndon Johnson

13.
"It depends on what the meaning of the words 'is' is."

Donald Trump	Gerald Ford	Bill Clinton

14.
"I think that gay marriage should be between a man and a woman."

Donald Trump	Arnold Schwarzenegger	Ted Kennedy

15.		
(To a wheelchair-bound man) "Stand up, Chuck. Let 'em see ya."		
Joe Biden	Sarah Palin	Mike Pence

16.		
"Well, if I ever ran for office, I'd do better as a Democrat than as a Republican - and that's not because I'd be more liberal, because I'm conservative. But the working guy would elect me. He likes me. When I walk down the street, those cabbies start yelling out their windows."		
Arnold Schwarzenegger	Mitt Romney	Donald Trump

17.		
"We do know of certain knowledge that he [Osama Bin Laden] is either in Afghanistan, or in some other country, or dead."		
Barack Obama	Donald Rumsfeld	George W. Bush

18.		
"I love California, I practically grew up in Phoenix."		
Dan Quayle	Mike Pence	Donald Trump

19.

"My fear is that the whole island [Guam] will become so overly populated that it will tip over and capsize."		
Dan Quayle	Hank Johnson	Bernie Sanders

20.

"The Holocaust was an obscene period in our nation's history. I mean in this century's history. But we all lived in this century. I didn't live in this century."		
Dan Quayle	George W. Bush	Donald Trump

Answers

1. George W. Bush
2. Ronald Reagan
3. Barack Obama
4. George W. Bush
5. Rudy Giuliani
6. Dan Quayle
7. Donald Rumsfeld
8. John Kerry
9. George H.W. Bush
10. Karen Handel

11. Jeb Bush
12. Richard Nixon
13. Bill Clinton
14. Arnold Schwarzenegger
15. Joe Biden
16. Donald Trump
17. Donald Rumsfeld
18. Dan Quayle
19. Hank Johnson
20. Dan Quayle

"The Imaginary Debate"

WHO CAN SHOUT THE LOUDEST?

According to *Atlantic* journalist Jonathan Haidt, the past decade of American politics has been "uniquely stupid". And who'd really disagree with him?

The 2010s and 2020s have seen both sides of American politics become more radicalized and less nuanced. The upshot of this is that political debates are absolutely useless. I mean it! You just try to agree with a Democrat student nowadays, it's almost impossible. It's not all their fault either – it's everyone's!

In a world where **all** Democrats are naïve nanny-state communists and **all** Republicans are racist queer-bashing fascists, how can anyone get their point across in a well-meaning manner?

Is it the end of democracy as we know it? Perhaps. Does it make for some excellently stupid social media posts and arguments? Absolutely.

This chapter is all about our most excellent public forum, the Internet, and is a chance to show off some of the best/worst jokes, points, arguments, statements, and all round silly stuff from its short but exciting history.

Some people are edgy. Some people are funny. Some people are both.

From X, 7/27/2020

"Damn North Korea has so much propaganda, anyway let's binge watch another tv show about the CIA saving the world."

There is no reason for you to be broke in the US, Mom! The smart man on TikTok told me so!

From TikTok, 2021

"There is no reason for you to be broke in the United States! Starting salary at most fast food restaurants is $10 per hour. If you work two full-time jobs at fast-food restaurants, you can bring in $700 per week!

Keep this up for two years and you'll be able to put away $20k per minimum each year! Put that into a quadplex or triplex, putting down a 3.5% down payment and rent out the other rooms.

In just two years you can bring in several thousand dollars a month, all from working at a fast food place.

There is **no** reason for you to be broke in the United States."

Is it time to tell all Millennials that Europe is mostly made up of Capitalist countries?

From X, 2021.

"Millennials don't hear socialism & think about the USSR or the Cold War.

We hear socialism & think about Canada *[not socialist]*, Switzerland *[not socialist]*, healthcare *[not socialist]*, social security *[not socialist]*, affordable college *[not socialist]*, & affordable housing *[not socialist]*.

Big *[and wrong]* generational difference!"

It's standard practice to make sure that politicians aren't lying, guys.

From X, 2020, post-Biden inauguration

"So weird, not having to fact-check a Presidential speech."
Reply: "We, uh, still have to do that."

So, one-party state? Reminds me of a certain Austrian gentleman who ruled Germany in the 1930s... Hmm...

From Reddit/r/politics, 2020

"It's not just Trump. All Republicans must go!"

You can't just say what you want... Can you?

From nextdoor.com, 2023

"Transvestites committed 25% of mass shootings in the last 4 years. They make up less than 0.5% of the population."

Reply: "You literally just made that up."

The BEST thing. Is it really the BEST thing?

From Rep. Steve Stockman, Twitter, 2013

"The best thing about the Earth is if you poke holes in it oil and gas come out."

Is it sexist to want war to end?

TikTok, about Kamala Harris' ordering of drone strikes.

"Genuine question: What's wrong with drone strikes?"

Reply: "This just screams misogyny!"

I dunno man,
I always got on with you.

THE GREAT DEBATE: TRIDEN OR BUMP?

Now look. Regardless of whether you're a "Trumpian" Republican, or whether you're after a politician who **wasn't** in *Home Alone 2*, you have to admit the man is hilarious. He's just funny! Both when he's trying to be and when he's not trying to be.

Equally funny for the same-but-different reasons is his running mate, Joe Biden! Somehow he's still the most likely Democrat to be voted in as President, probably because he was around when the United States gained its independence.

In this section, you'll be presented with tweets, quotes, and other such words from our favorite octogenarian presidents, and it will be your job to label which one of them said (or typed at 3am) it! Good luck! The answers are at the end of the chapter!

A. "I will be phenomenal to the women. I mean, I want to help women."

Trump or Biden?

B. "I have a great relationship with African Americans, as you possibly have heard. I just have great respect for them. And they like me. I like them."

Brump or Tiden?

C. "We are America, second to none, and we own the finish line. Don't forget it."

Frump or Spiden?

D. "Despite the constant negative press, covfefe."

Whump or Briden?

E. "We hold these truths to be self evident: all men and women are created, by the, you know the, you know the thing."

Mump or Kiden?

F. "Poor kids are just as bright and just as talented as white kids"

Plump or Tiden?

G. "If you looked at Saddam Hussein, he killed terrorists, I'm not saying he was an angel, but this guy killed terrorists.

Blump or Widen?

H. "Why don't you say something nice instead of being a smart ass all the time?"

Scrump or Niden?

I. "His mom lived in Long Island for 10 years or so, God rest her soul, and, er, although she's, wait – your mom's still alive. It was your dad who's passed. God bless her soul. I gotta get this straight."

Drump or Siden?

J. "Look, John's last-minute economic plan does nothing to tackle the number one job facing the middle class, and it happens to be... a three letter word: jobs, J-O-B-S.

Grump or Hidin'?

K. "The concept of shaking hands is absolutely terrible, and statistically I've been proven right."

Snump or Ciden?

L. "As a kid, I was making a building with blocks in our playroom. I didn't have enough. So I asked my younger brother if I could borrow some of his. He said, 'Okay, but you have to give them back when you're done.' I used all of my blocks, then all of his blocks, and when I was done I had a great building, which I then glued together. [He] never did get those blocks back."

Rump or Ridin'?

M. "In Delaware, the largest growth of population is Indian Americans, moving from India. You cannot go to a 7/11 or a Dunkin' Donuts unless you have a slight Indian accent. I'm not joking."

Stump or Stridin'?

N. "Nobody has better respect for intelligence than Donald Trump."

Bump or Guidin'?

Answers

Trump	Biden
A, B, D, G, K, L, N	C, E, F, H, I, J, M

"The Great Robbery"

"Hey, watch out! That guy's taking all your money!"

WOKING THE BEAR OF CINEMA

Here we go again! Back to *Woking the Bear,* but this time we're focusing on the great and wide world of cinema.

Movies have titillated for more than a century, with the art-form remaining one of the more dominant forms to this day. But riddle me this... when you consider the greats, such as *Citizen Kane, The Godfather, The Shawshank Redemption, The Nutty Professor 2*... wouldn't they have had a far better impact if they were more politically correct?

Well, Dr. Wokenstein thinks so, and they're (gender neutral, you're welcome) here to re-write some of the great cinematic pieces in order to make them more inclusive, and to align them more with sensitive Middle America.

Titanic (1997)

In the 1997 film *Titanic*, directed by James Cameron, a passionate romance unfolds between Jack Dawson, a penniless artist, and Rose DeWitt Bukater, a young aristocrat, aboard the ill-fated RMS *Titanic*.

The couple's love faces numerous obstacles, including the class divide and the impending tragedy of the ship sinking. Against the backdrop of the historical disaster, Jack and Rose's love story becomes a timeless tale of heartbreak and sacrifice.

Dr. Wokenstein's edit:

In the 1997 film *Titanic*, directed by James Cameron, we examine the perspective of the iceberg involved in the collision.

A powerful metaphor for the brutal nature of humanity and our disregard for the climate, the piece now highlights the feelings of the iceberg. The viewers go away thinking about the tragedy at the loss of a big lump of ice. The whole love angle gets dumped.

Mad Max: Fury Road (2015)

Mad Max: Fury Road, directed by George Miller, is a high-octane post-apocalyptic action film. In a desolate wasteland, the enigmatic Max teams up with Furiosa, a fierce warrior, as they embark on a high-speed journey to escape the tyrannical rule of Immortan Joe.

The relentless pursuit by Joe's warlord army leads to a spectacular and explosive car chase across the desert, where survival depends on trust, resourcefulness, and a quest for freedom in a world gone mad.

Dr. Wokenstein's Edit:

Mad Max: Fury Road, directed by George Miller, is a powerful, high-octane exploration for renewable energy sources.

Max teams up with Furiosa who kindly explain to Immortan Joe that the use of petrol is bad for the planet. Joe, who never knew of the damaging impact of fossil fuels, commissions the world's greatest scientists to work on Electric Vehicle technology – dubbing Max as "Mad" because he's so hell-bent on saving the planet.

The movie becomes a powerful message of love and ends with the petrol cars being successfully converted into Prius hybrids.

Fight Club (1999)

In *Fight Club*, directed by David Fincher, an unnamed narrator struggling with insomnia forms an unconventional friendship with the charismatic and anarchistic Tyler Durden.

Together, they create an underground fight club as a form of male bonding and rebellion against societal norms. As the club evolves into something more sinister, the narrative takes unexpected twists, delving into themes of identity, consumerism, and the consequences of unchecked rebellion, leading to a mind-bending climax.

Dr. Wokenstein's Edit:

In *Fight Club*, directed by David Fincher, an unnamed narrator struggling with insomnia forms an unconventional friendship with the charismatic, gender-fluid Tyler Durden.

Together, they create an underground safe-space support group, where men are free to discuss their emotions openly, challenging toxic masculinity, fostering mental health awareness, and encouraging discussions around modern gender identity.

The movie culminates in mind-bending leftie acceptance and broad liberal appeal, which upsets no one and makes no statement beyond "be nice."

The Dark Knight Rises (2012)

In *The Dark Knight Rises*, directed by Christopher Nolan, Gotham City faces a new threat as the masked terrorist Bane emerges, plotting to destroy the city.

Retired and reclusive, Bruce Wayne must don the Batman mantle again to confront Bane and protect Gotham.

As a complex web of alliances and betrayals unfolds, Batman's physical and mental limits are tested in an epic showdown that challenges not only the hero's legacy but the very survival of Gotham itself.

Dr. Wokenstein's Edit:

In *The Dark Knight Rises*, directed by Christopher Nolan, masked eco-terrorist Bane emerges, orchestrating a series of disruptive events and demonstrations.

In the chaos that ensues, Bane restores calm to Gotham City, by turning the struggling metropolis into a revolutionary yoga retreat where citizens find inner peace through meditation and wellness.

The residents grow to resent Batman's "hands-on" approach to crime and ostracize him from society unless he learns to align his chakras.

The Wizard of Oz (1939)

The Wizard of Oz follows Dorothy, a young girl swept away to the magical land of Oz in a tornado.

Determined to return home, she embarks on a journey with her companions—the Scarecrow, Tin Man, and Cowardly Lion—to seek the help of the Wizard of Oz.

Along the Yellow Brick Road, they encounter challenges, face the Wicked Witch of the West, and discover that the power to fulfill their desires lies within themselves.

Dr. Wokenstein's Edit:

...Okay, this is pretty woke, but maybe we make Dorothy black?

Jaws (1975)

In Steven Spielberg's *Jaws*, a small coastal town is terrorized by a great white shark, prompting Police Chief Martin Brody, oceanographer Matt Hooper, and grizzled shark hunter Quint to join forces in a perilous quest to eliminate the deadly threat.

As the suspenseful hunt unfolds at sea, the trio faces escalating danger and tension, culminating in a gripping battle of man versus nature. *Jaws* became a classic, setting the standard for the summer blockbuster and forever changing the way audiences perceive the ocean.

Dr. Wokenstein's Edit:

Despite a tricky beginning, where the titular shark in *Jaws* attacks swimmers off the coast of the small island, he turns it around and changes as a shark.

Moving onto plant-based, non-human alternatives and protein shakes, the shark becomes a protector of summer on the island.

He becomes an ambassador for the island and for the symbiotic nature of life between animals and humankind.

"Call of Duty: Modern Warfare 5"

★
THE MODERN SOCIALIST

The words "Socialist" and "Socialism" get thrown around a lot. Realistically, most people who use these words don't really understand what they mean and just say them because they make them *sound* like they know what they're talking about.

Socialism is really about believing in a society where equality reigns and business is owned by everyone, rather than a rich few.

Sounds quite nice. But in reality, Socialist countries tend to become dictatorships and corrupt. So, seeing the similarities, it's no wonder that a growing number of Americans now identify as Socialists!

In this chapter, we'll have a laugh at Socialists, Socialism and enjoy a few proper jokes.

Comrade President! Our people are dying of hunger. Do something!

Release a statement. We are radically reducing the number of people who live below the poverty line. Success!

***

Jokes about Socialism are only good if everybody gets them.

***

Q: What is Socialism?

A: A system which bravely and innovatively conquers barriers that wouldn't be present in any other system.

***

A sign that adorns a Soviet prison library reads:

"We're sorry, but we don't have the book you wanted. But we do have the author!"

***

What is a Russian hamburger?

Two bread tickets with a meat ticket between them.

Q: How many Communists do you need to change a lightbulb?

A: Two hundred.

Ten to create a five-year plan to accomplish the task.

Ten to set up a state-owned factory to produce lightbulbs.

Twenty to work in the factory.

Fifty to establish a union and run the union paper.

Ninety-nine to create a campaign proving the original lightbulb was destroyed by Capitalists.

And one to nip over to America and buy a lightbulb.

***

Q: Why did the Socialist start a gardening club?

A: They wanted to cultivate a grassroots movement.

***

Q: How does a Socialist party?

A: By splitting the bill equally.

***

Q: How many Socialists does it take to change a lightbulb?

A: None. The lightbulb contains the seeds of its own revolution.

Q: Why do Socialists hate math?

A: Because none of the numbers is equal!

***

In Soviet Russia, a man is walking along the street, and he spits on the floor. A policeman approaches him and says, "It's best not to talk politics, Comrade".

***

Two Russian intellectuals are discussing the destiny of the country.

One says, "What do you think the future of Russia will look like in the next three years?"

The other says, "I don't know. I have no idea what our past will look like in three years."

***

Child: When I grow up, I want to be a Socialist!

Father: You can't do both.

***

"I'm a Socialist drinker."

The bartender chuckled and asked me, "Don't you mean a *social* drinker?"

"No, I only drink when someone else is paying."

Q: Where does a Socialist bird lay its eggs?

A: In a Communest.

***

Q: Why do Socialists only drink decaffeinated tea?

A: Because proper tea is theft.

***

Two nudist Socialists are sitting on a porch. One turns to the other and asks, "Have you read Marx?"

The other says, "Yes, I think it's these wicker chairs."

***

A Socialist, a Marxist, and a Postmodernist walk into a bar.

The bouncer turns to them and says, "Sorry guys, come back when you're 21".

***

My now-ex girlfriend has been sent to jail for plotting a radical Socialist coup.

I guess I should have paid attention to all the red flags.

***

Did you hear the one about having lunch in a Socialist country? Sorry, you wouldn't get it.

Q: How do you know someone is a Socialist?

A: Don't worry, they'll tell you.

***

Capitalism is dancing at the edge of the abyss.

Socialism, of course, is one step ahead of them.

***

Q: What do you call a funny person who is a Socialist?

A: A commie-dian.

***

Q: Why are Socialist school teachers so deliberately disorganized?

A: They love to see the class struggle.

***

Q: What did Socialists use to light their homes before candles?

A: Electricity.

***

I asked my cat who his favorite Socialist is. He just looked at me and said, "Mao."

A regional Communist Party meeting is held to celebrate the anniversary of the Great October Socialist Revolution. The Chairman gives a speech: "Dear Comrades! Let's look at the amazing achievements of our Party after the revolution.

"For example, Maria here. Who was she before the revolution? An illiterate peasant; she had but one dress and no shoes. And now? She is an exemplary milkmaid known throughout the entire region.

"Or look at Ivan Andreev. He was the poorest man in this village; he had no horse, no cow, not even an ax. And now? He is a tractor driver with two pairs of shoes!

"Or Trofim Semenovich Alekseev – he was a nasty hooligan, a drunk, and a dirty gadabout. Nobody would trust him with as much as a snowdrift in wintertime as he would steal anything he could get his hands on. And now he's Secretary of the Party Committee!"

***

You can make a Capitalist poor and they'll still believe in Capitalism. However, if you make a Socialist rich, you'll have a new Capitalist.

***

I scored well in my Socialism exam last week In fact I got top Marx.

***

Q: How do you get people dancing in a Socialist country?

A: Tape a piece of bread to the ceiling.

Q: What do you call a Socialist horse?

A: Trotsky

***

Real Socialism: Waiting on the breadline.

Joke Socialism: Waiting on the punchline.

"Crisis Management"

"I'm sorry but they moved to Florida, they knew the risks.
We can't be bailing them out just because they've finally realized
that they have DeSantis down there."

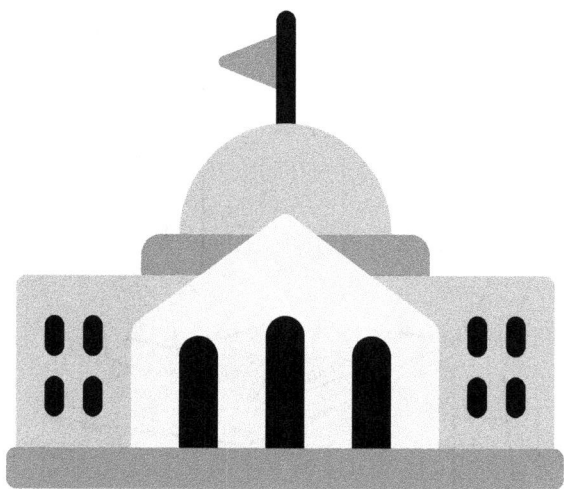

SERIOUS STORIES FROM THE SERIOUS SENATE

The US Senate is, for some, the cornerstone of global democracy. Like the great debating halls of Ancient Greece, the country's brightest and best come together to vote fairly for the good of its citizens.

Oh wait.

Much unlike the debating halls of Ancient Greece, the country's most power-hungry and petty come together to argue, bicker, and filibuster so no real work can get done.

The US Senate is a serious place, but it's had its fair share of downright silly moments over the decades. In this chapter, you'll get a chance to read about *some* of them! Enjoy.

Storm Thurmond's Filibuster of 1957

In the historic filibuster of 1957, Strom Thurmond spoke for a staggering 24 hours and 18 minutes against the Civil Rights Act.

As the clock ticked, Thurmond covered everything from his grandmother's cat to his favorite barbecue joint. Even the Senate pages started measuring their lives in "Thurmond Time." The record-setting filibuster became a lesson in both political endurance and the senator's eclectic range of topics – proving that when Thurmond got going, even the most dedicated viewers were reaching for the remote.

History would paint Thurmond in a bad light as the Civil Rights Act has universally been agreed to be a good thing, but it goes some way to showing the immense creativity that some of these politicians hold.

The Inhofe Snowball, 2015

Jim Inhofe has somehow managed to survive one of the most tone-deaf demonstrations of all time, enduring in the Senate until 2023 at the grand old age of 89.

There has been debate for a long time over whether or not climate change is serious, man-made, or something we should be concerned with. What's undeniable is that the planet is getting warmer over time, it's just whether or not we humans are able to do anything about it.

In February 2015, Inhofe delivered the ultimate "There's no such thing as climate change" – or he thought he did anyway.

Inhofe was addressing the Senate, when he reached down and picked up a large snowball. He proudly announced to the room that, "It's very, very cold" outside, and that the snow proved that global warming is simply a myth.

Inhofe called out, "Here, Mr. President, catch this!" and threw the snowball onto the Senate floor. Inhofe adopted a cocky smile and ended his speech, thus making himself look like the most out-of-touch moron there's ever been.

He may have a career longer than most people get to live, but it's defined by this one moment, and it's glorious.

The Filibuster that wasn't technically a Filibuster

In 2013, Barack Obama was pushing through what many would call his "legacy" bill: The Affordable Care Act, aka Obamacare.

The Act had received full funding and was going to be passed, but that didn't stop Sen. Ted Cruz from drawing attention away from the bill. Cruz addressed the Senate for an impressive 21 hours, in a clear effort to derail proceedings, or perhaps to just annoy the President.

In order to fill out the full time, Cruz would veer off topic regularly. He'd discuss his favorite burgers, Ashton Kutcher's best acting, the movie *Psycho*, and the occasional Darth Vader impression.

Without a doubt the highlight was a full recital of Dr Suess' *Green Eggs & Ham*, which he claimed he was reading for his two daughters.

Why they'd be watching I don't know. I mean, how many children would like to watch their father display signs of early-onset dementia?

Heyyyy, Senator, Senator, SWING, Senator!

In a rare display of bipartisanship, the Washington boys' club found common ground on a sunny summer day in 2010 — courtesy of baseball.

The Senate's majority and minority leaders set aside six minutes of official Senate time to swap tales and gossip about the Washington Nationals. The buzz was due to star pitcher Stephen Strasburg's dazzling Major League debut with 14 strikeouts, setting a team record. Harry M. Reid, the then Majority Leader, lauded Strasburg, and Mitch McConnell, the Minority Leader, echoed the praise.

Bantering back and forth, McConnell cheekily suggested, "What one could conclude from this is that next year, when the Senate is not in session in the evening, both the Republican and Democratic leaders will be at baseball games."

They may not be able to agree on much, but Republicans and Democrats are always able to agree on men playing a (let's be honest now) quite boring sport.

"A true Political Rally!"

LET'S GET POLITICAL! POLITICAL!

Look, there's a litany of amazing political jokes out there that don't quite fit into any of the chapters of this book. They're just generally great politics jokes, so we need somewhere to put them – which is here.

In this chapter you'll find a few puns, jokes about diplomats, and general politics fun.

You can even enjoy this chapter with your Democrat neighbor, Joe! Even if he'll say "Well, actually..." about a dozen times.

Q: Why don't I tell jokes about the Civil War?

A: Because I "General Lee" don't find them funny.

***

Q: What do computers do when mimicking the dancing moves of the vice presidents?

A: They follow the "Al-Gore-Rhythm"

***

Ban Pre-Shredded Cheese!

Make America Grate Again.

***

War doesn't determine who is right, only who is left.

***

Politics.

Poly = Many

Tics = Blood sucking parasites.

***

A Liberal, a Moderate, and a Conservative walk into a bar.

The bartender says, "Hey Mitt, what can I get you?"

Three surgeons are discussing what the easiest kind of person to operate on is.

"Oh, it's got to be electricians," says the First. "Everything inside is color coded."

"Nonsense, definitely librarians," counters the Second. "They keep everything alphabetized."

"Please, everyone knows politicians are the easiest," explains the Third. "There are no guts, no heart, no balls, no brains, and no spine. Plus, the head and the butt are interchangeable!"

***

"Suppose you were an idiot. Now suppose you were a member of Congress. But I repeat myself."

Mark Twain

A curious Boy asks his Father:

"What is Politics?"

Father answers:

"It's very simple! You see, I bring in the money, so I'm Big Business. Your Mother spends the money, so she's the Government.

"Your Grandfather sees to it that everything is managed in an orderly way. So, he's the Law.

"Our Maid is the Working Class.

"Everything revolves around your interests, so you're the People. Your little baby brother represents the Future."

The Boy has to think it over. That night he hears his little brother crying due to a dirty diaper. He doesn't know what to do, so he goes to his parents' bedroom. There his Mother is sound asleep. He goes to the bedroom of the Maid, but his father is there making love to her while his Grandfather is watching through the window.

Nobody notices the Boy and he returns to his bed.

The next day his Father asks him:

"So, can you now explain to me what politics is?"

The boy says:

"Yes, it's all become clear to me!

"Big Business screws the Working Class while the Law watches and the Government sleeps. The People are ignored, and the future lies waiting deep in excrement."

Q: You know why fish are so political?

A: They're always taking debate.

***

I used to really enjoy political jokes. But too many of them got elected.

***

Q: What do you call a person who's an expert in American culture and politics?

A: A European.

***

I hate when political candidates put their signs up in my front yard! Who the hell is Foreclosure?

***

If Trump wins the next election, I will leave the United States.

If Biden wins the next election, I will leave the United States.

I'm not making a statement; I just want to travel.

***

Politicians are like sperm.

Only one in a million turn out to be human.

Q: What's the difference between politicians and thieves?

A: Thieves steal your money and run, while politicians run and then steal your money.

***

Two high-ranking politicians visit a school. The more mature statesman goes over the expenses and decides to make adjustments to cut costs.

"The lunch portions are too big. Cut them in half. The Internet connection is too fast. There are too many computers."

After that, they go to a preschool. Again, the expenses are too great for the elderly politician.

"The lunch portions are too big, half them. There are too many toys as well, let's get rid of those."

After the preschool, they go to a prison.

"The lunch portions are too small, and the selection is too limited. Get faster broadband and more comfortable beds. The TVs are too old, what is this 1970? Get a few consoles in here as well!"

The junior politician is appalled and baffled. He leans in and whispers to the old man, "Are you mad? We just cut costs in schools and preschools, and now you do this?"

The statesman replies, "My friend, we will never go to school or preschool again. But we're one leaked email away from ending up here..."

A prominent politician was visiting a village, and asked what their needs were.

"We have two basic needs, sir!" replied the villager.

"Firstly, we have a hospital, but there's no doctor."

On hearing this, the politician pulled out his cellphone, and spoke for a while to someone on the other line. After a time, he hung up and reassured the villager that the doctor would be there the very next day. He then asked what the second problem was.

"Secondly, sir, there is no cell phone coverage anywhere in this village."

***

A Republican Senator and a Democratic Senator are drowning and you can only save one. Do you...

A: Have lunch

B: Take a nap

***

I parked my car outside of the White House. "Sir, you can't park here", said a cop. "This is where our politicians work."

"Don't worry," I responded. "I've locked it."

***

Q: What's the most unfair thing about American politics?

A: We get fifty choices for Miss America, but only two for President.

In America, prison reform is a political issue.

In Russia, political reform is a prison issue.

***

A farmer saw a plane full of politicians crash near his farm. When the police arrived, they asked the farmer what happened.

The farmer told them, "They crashed near my farm and I buried all of them!"

One of the policemen asked with shock, "Are you sure they were all dead?"

"Well, some of them were screaming "We are still alive!", but you know these politicians and how much they lie."

***

A little boy asks his mother what the difference is between a Democrat and a Republican.

The mother thinks hard and comes up with an explanation for her son:

"A Democrat is like that very nice aunt you have that always promises to take you to Disneyland, but something always comes up and they never actually take you.

"A Republican, however, is like a grumpy uncle. Every time you ask him about Disneyland, he says absolutely not because there's not enough money. Later on you find out he went without you."

Kid: Dad, when I grow up, I want to be in politics.

Dad: Are you insane? Have you completely lost your mind? Are you a moron?

Kid: Forget it, there are too many entry requirements.

***

I remember when Halloween was the scariest night of the year. Now it's election night.

***

The NSA: A government organization that actually listens to you!

***

People who want to share their religious or political views with you almost never want you to share yours with them.

***

Instead of giving a politician the keys to the city, it might be better to change the locks!

***

Q: What's the difference between baseball and politics?

A: In baseball you're out if you're caught stealing.

"Poli-ticking the box."

"Just remember, I stand for _____
and I love the _____ community.
You mean the most to me so I will
make sure I _____ taxes and _____
the security presence near your schools.
My favorite part of the _____ community,
is the _____ and I'm looking forward
to working more with you in the future.

There you go, just pop in whichever
group we're pretending
to care about this week."

---★---

FAKE NEWS! OR NOT.

"Fake News!"

The phrase gained a certain amount of legitimacy when, in 2017, Collins announced that it was their Word of the year.

It came against the backdrop of a year of Donald Trump decrying what he saw as incorrect information in the build up to his inauguration and during his presidency.

The near constant calls of "fake news" made it difficult to work out exactly what news was real and what news was fake. Which brings us to this chapter!

Here you will come up against twenty news News headlines. Some are fake and some are true – can you identify which is which? The answers are at the end. Don't cheat!

1. MAN CHANGES NAME TO CAPTAIN FANTASTIC FASTER THAN SUPERMAN, SPIDERMAN, BATMAN, WOLVERINE, HULK AND THE FLASH COMBINED

Fake News or Trews?

2. MAN HAS EX-GIRLFRIEND REMOVED FROM HIS MEMORY, DOCTOR'S HAIL THIS NEW TECHNOLOGY DESPITE EMOTIONAL RAMIFICATIONS

Fake News or Trews?

3. WOMAN CLAIMS TO HAVE GIVEN BIRTH TO PET DOG

Fake News or Trews?

4. MAN TURNS INTO LOBSTER

Fake News or Trews?

5. WOMAN CALLS 911 TO REPORT MISSING CHICKEN NUGGETS

Fake News or Trews?

6. TEXAN MAN KILLS HIS FATHER AND MARRIES HIS MOTHER IN HORRIFIC SCENE

Fake News or Trews?

7. MEAT RAINS FROM THE SKY, BAFFLES KENTUCKY LOCALS

Fake News or Trews?

8. MAN MISTAKES WIFE FOR HAT

Fake News or Trews?

9. CHIMP WINS PRIMARIES IN SOUTH-EAST ASIA

Fake News or Trews?

10. TOWN CHANGES NAME TO DISH, IN ORDER TO CASH IN ON FREE SATELLITE TELEVISION

Fake News or Trews?

11. MYSTERIOUS PHANTOM BARBER STRIKES AGAIN, CUTS HAIR OF UNSUSPECTING MISSISSIPPI RESIDENTS

Fake News or Trews?

12. WOMAN DIES BECAUSE OF HORRIFIC LONG-SCARFCAR ACCIDENT

Fake News or Trews?

13. MAN USES CORRUPT PRIEST TO MARRY A JAR OF STICK INSECTS IN BIZARRE CEREMONY IN NEW ENGLAND

Fake News or Trews?

14. WORLD WAR TWO INVENTOR ACCIDENTALLY INVENTS SILLY PUTTY, IN A MOVE THAT ALLIED COMMANDERS CALL "UPSETTING"

Fake News or Trews?

15. MAN IS FOUND TO USE 43% OF HIS BRAIN, POSSESSING AN IQ AT LEAST ABOVE 310

Fake News or Trews?

16. WORLD HEALTH ORGANIZATION CONFIRMS THE EXISTENCE OF ZOMBIES IN STUNNING NEW REPORT

Fake News or Trews?

17. SHARKS LAUNCHED INTO SKY BY FEROCIOUS TORNADO

Fake News or Trews?

18. WI-FI BANNED IN WEST VIRGINIAN TOWN

Fake News or Trews?

19. BRITISH CHILD, MAXWELL, GOES ON HORRENDOUS RAMPAGE WITH A SILVER HAMMER, KILLS SEVERAL

Fake News or Trews?

20. MONTANA WOMAN CALLS POLICE TO COMPLAIN ABOUT THE QUALITY OF METH THAT SHE'D JUST BOUGHT

Fake News or Trews?

Answers

1. True. What other context do you need?

2. Fake News! This is the basic premise behind *Eternal Sunshine of the Spotless Mind.*

3. Fake News! Or at least, I hope it is.

4. Fake News! I mean come on now, you must have known this was the plot to *The Lobster* from 2015.

5. True! McDonalds had run out of Nuggets, so she phoned... the police.

6. Fake News! This is the famous Ancient Greek story of *Oedipus.* Look it up!

7. True! In Bath County, Kentucky in the year of 1876, chunks of red meat fell from the sky!

8. True! Neurologist Oliver Sacks, in 1985, wrote about a patient who had a bizarre visual agnosia and mistook his own wife for a hat.

9. Fake News! No – but if it were true, then we could use the pun "Primateries" which is funny.

10. True! Clark, Texas, changed its name to "Dish" in 2005 as part of a deal with the Dish Network satellite TV service. Remember, this was before streaming; they'll be kicking themselves now.

11. True! In Pascagoula, Mississippi, a mysterious night barber was suspected of breaking into people's homes and cutting their hair.

12. True! This was the famous case of the celebrated dancer Isadora Duncan, who was wearing a long scarf that became tangled in the wheels of the car she was traveling in in France.

13. Fake News! Stick Insects are famously non-committal.

14. True! The inventor, James Wright, was attempting to find a substitute for rubber, which was in short supply during WW2.

15. Fake News! The common misconception that we only use "a certain percentage" of our brain is nonsense. We use a lot of our brain in our everyday lives, why on Earth would we only use 10%? I mean come on.

16. Fake News! And real fake news too. The WHO released this as a prank, to capitalize on the huge popularity of zombie shows in entertainment. (It's worth saying they did this before the world shut down due to a virus).

17. Fake News! This is the plot to *Sharknado*, which is about as far away from "truth" as you could get.

18. True! Green Bank, West Virginia banned Wi-Fi and cellphones in order to protect a gigantic radio telescope from interference in 2010.

19. Fake News! This is a reference to The Beatles' song, *Maxwell's Silver Hammer* which is about... well, that.

20. True! In 2017, a Montana woman phoned 911 to complain about the meth she'd just purchased. Yeah, it's never a *good* idea to tell the police you've broken the law.

"Don't worry, the CIA disconnected this button
the moment our president's started collecting their pensions."

DEMOCRATS II: BIDEN YER TIME

We're back again! For one last bout of mocking the Democrats.

In this book, you've had a chance to laugh at politicians, politics, bonkers news stories, woke-ness, stories from the Senate and all sorts. So why don't we take one last swipe at this country's most well-meaning, yet least able, political party?

Those darn democRATS!

"I am not a member of any organized political party, I am a Democrat." – Will Rogers

***

The Republicans have a genius plan to make the Democrats sound stupid.

Operation "Let them talk" is now well under way.

***

Q: What does Bill say to Hillary after great sex?

A: "Honey, I'll be home in 15 minutes."

***

Q: Why should Democrats be buried 100 feet deep?

A: Because deep down, they're really good people.

***

A party of Democrats was climbing in the Alps. After several hours they became hopelessly lost, so one of them studied the map for some time. He turned it upside down, twisted it about, and set his sight on distant landmarks. He glanced at his compass, and finally the sun.

At last, he said, "Okay, see that big mountain over there?"

"Yes?" answered the others eagerly.

"Well, according to the map, we're standing on top of it."

When Albert Einstein died, he met three people in the line outside the Pearly Gates.

To pass the time, he enquired about their IQs.

The first replied that they had an IQ of 190.

"Wonderful!" exclaimed Einstein. "We can discuss the contribution made by Ernest Rutherford to atomic physics and my theory of general relativity."

The second answered that they had an IQ of 150. "Good," said Einstein. "I look forward to discussing the role of Gingrich's Contract with America legislation in moving us into the twenty-first century."

The third person mumbled 50.

Einstein paused, and then asked, "What was it like being vice-president, Mr. Gore?"

***

Q: What is a recent Democrat graduate's usual question in his first job?

A: Would you like fries with that, sir?

The National Institute of Health (NIH) announced that they were going to start using Democrats instead of rats in their experiments.

Naturally, the Democratic National Committee was outraged and filed suit, but NIH presented several compelling reasons for the switch:

1. NIH lab assistants became very attached to their rats. This emotional involvement was very unlikely to happen in Democrats.

2. Democrats breed faster.

3. Democrats are much cheaper to care for and PETA won't object on ethical grounds to any experiment.

4. There are some things even rats won't do.

Unfortunate drawbacks: It will be difficult to apply results to human beings.

***

Santa Claus, the Tooth Fairy, a conservative Democrat, and an old drunk are walking down the street together when they simultaneously spot a $100 bill on the floor.

They leap to it at the same time – but who gets it?

A: The old drunk of course, the other three are mythological creatures.

A wealthy Democrat had a summer house in the Maine woods. Each summer he'd invite a different friend to spend a week or two there with him.

On one occasion, he invited a man from the Czech Republic to stay with him. They had a splendid time in the country - rising early and living in the great outdoors.

Early one morning, they went out to pick berries for their morning breakfast. As they went around the berry patch, along came two huge bears.

The Democrat dashed for cover. His friend wasn't so lucky, and the male bear reached him and swallowed him whole. The Democrat ran back to his car, drove to town as fast has he could, and got the sheriff. The sheriff grabbed his rifle and dashed back to the berry patch with the Democrat. Sure enough, both bears were still there.

"He's in THAT one!" cried the Democrat, pointing to the male. The sheriff looked at the bears, and without batting an eye, leveled his gun, took careful aim, and shot the female.

"What did you do that for?!" exclaimed the Democrat. "I said he was in the other bear!"

"Yep," said the sheriff, "but would you believe a Democrat who told you that the Czech was in the male?"

***

Democrats, like diapers, need to be changed.

Often for the same reason.

Q: How many Democrats does it take to change a lightbulb?

A: It's irrelevant. They still don't know they're in the dark.

***

Q: What's a Republican?

A: A Democrat who makes it through adolescence.

***

Q: How many Republicans does it take to raise your taxes?

A: None. The Democrats do that.

***

Q: What's the difference between an intelligent Democrat and Bigfoot?

A: Bigfoot has been spotted.

***

They should build the wall with Hillary's emails, because no one seems to be able to get over them.

"Speeches then and now"

1933

2024

NO TIME LIKE THE PRESIDENT II

I know we've already had a selection of presidential jokes, but frankly there have been so many stupid presidents that we could write a book of them!

So, to see out the last section of this terrific collection of bizarre jokes, we're going to have a few pages of presidential proportions. Enjoy jokes about some of our silliest leaders and fantastically funny quotes from some of the brightest!

When George W. Bush was president, I was genuinely convinced that he was going to destroy the world because he was hungry and pressed the "lunch" button.

***

Bill Clinton, George W. Bush, and George Washington are on a sinking ship.

As the boat sinks, George Washington heroically shouts, "Save the women!"

George Bush hysterically yells out, "Save me! Screw the women!"

Bill Clinton excitedly asks, "Do we have time?"

***

"It was absolutely involuntary. They sank my boat."

President John Kennedy.

(Answering a little boy who had asked him how he became a war hero.)

***

"Politics is supposed to be the second-oldest profession... and I have come to realize that it bears a very close resemblance to the first."

President Ronald Reagan.

***

"In my many years I have come to a conclusion that one useless man is a shame, two is a law firm, and three or more is a congress."

President John Adams.

An airplane was about to crash. There were four passengers on board, but only three parachutes.

The first passenger said, "I am LeBron James, the best NBA basketball player. The Lakers and my millions of fans need me, and I can't afford to die." So he took the first pack and left the plane.

The second passenger, George Bush, said, "I was the US president, and I was the smartest president in American history, so my people don't want me to die." He took the second pack and jumped out of the plane.

The third passenger, the Pope, said to the fourth passenger, a 10-year-old schoolboy, "My son, I am old and don't have many years left. You have more years ahead, so I will sacrifice my life and let you have the last parachute."

The little boy said, 'That's okay, Your Holiness, there's a parachute left for you. America's smartest president took my schoolbag"

The year is 2028 and the United States has elected the first woman, as well as the first Jewish president, Sarah Goldstein.

She calls up her mother a few weeks after Election Day and says, "So, Mom, I assume you'll be coming to my inauguration?"

"I don't think so. It's a ten-hour drive, your father isn't as young as he used to be, and my arthritis is acting up again."

"Don't worry about it, Mom, I'll send Air Force One to pick you up and take you home. And a limousine will pick you up at your door."

"I don't know. Everybody will be so fancy-schmantzy; what on earth would I wear?

Sarah replies, "I'll make sure you have a wonderful gown, custom-made by the best designer in New York."

"Honey," Mom complains, "you know I can't eat those rich foods you and your friends like to eat."

The president-to-be responds, "Don't worry, Mom. The entire affair is going to be handled by the best caterer in New York; kosher all the way, Mom, I really want you to come."

So, Mom reluctantly agrees, and on January 20, 2029, Sarah Goldstein is being sworn in as President of the United States. In the front row sits the new president's mother, who leans over to a senator sitting next to her and says, "You see that woman over there with her hand on the Torah, becoming President of the United States?"

The senator whispers back, "Yes, I do."

Mom says proudly, "Her brother is a doctor."

President Biden has called for a full legalization of marijuana.

Now it is up to Congress to call a joint session.

***

In 1992, while being interviewed by MTV, Bill Clinton was asked if he wore boxers or briefs. Clinton replied, "Boxers"

In 2008. US Magazine asked Obama, "Boxers or briefs?" Obama declined to answer the question.

Last week AARP asked Joe Biden, "Boxers or briefs?" Biden responded, "Depends."

The US president asked for estimates from contractors from different countries to paint the White House.

The Chinese contractor estimated $3 million.

The European contractor said the cost was $7 million.

The Pakistani contractor estimated $10 million.

The president asked the Chinese contractor, "How did you estimate three million dollars?"

The contractor replied, "1 million for paint, 1 million for labor, and 1 million for profit."

The president then asked the European contractor how he had reached seven million. He replied, "3 million in paint, 2 million in labor, 2 million in profit!"

The president then asked the Pakistani contractor how he'd estimated ten million. The Pakistani contractor said, "4 million for you, 3 million for me, the remaining 3 million will be given to the Chinese to paint."

The Pakistani contractor got the contract.

"How to change a Democrat's mind"

"Go and mug him at gunpoint for his wallet,
we'll see if he's so in favor of raising taxes then!"

PARTING WORDS

And so concludes this bizarre book, stuffed to the brim with useless stories and far more useful jokes! Sure to bring your dinner guests to their knees with laughter (and equally sure to upset your relatives) regale all with the words on these pages and become the most interesting person in the room!

This book was written at the start of 2024, just before the American election really took flight. At this stage, the outcome is unpredictable.

What is perhaps the greatest joke of all, however, is that it seems very likely that the American public will be about to vote for two candidates who have a combined age of more than 150. The exact same choice they had four years ago.

Here's hoping that the 2028 election will have new opportunities on both sides, and a chance for the American government to move away from the retirement village that it is becoming.

I hope you cast your vote well, listen to what your politicians have to say, and most importantly, listen to people that don't think the same as you. Test your own beliefs and you'll be far more informed. Knowing what policies you're voting against, as well as for, is crucial if you want to consider yourself "informed."

Here's to you, America! The whole world watches on with bated breath this year.

If you're reading this after 2024, then no spoilers please, don't tell me who won! There may yet be a chance that my 100,000/1 bet will come off and George Washington's skeleton might win it!

www.ingramcontent.com/pod-product-compliance
Lightning Source LLC
Chambersburg PA
CBHW060245030426
42335CB00014B/1599